EASY JAZZ FAVORITES

15 Selections For Young Jazz Ensembles

T0071590

Contents

HAL•LEONARD® CORPORATION
7777 W. BLUEMOUND RD. P.O. BOX 13819 MILWAUKEE, WI 53213

AIN'T MISBEHAVIN'

Words by ANDY RAZAF
Music by THOMAS WALLER and HARRY BROOKS
Arranged by BOB LOWDEN

PIANO

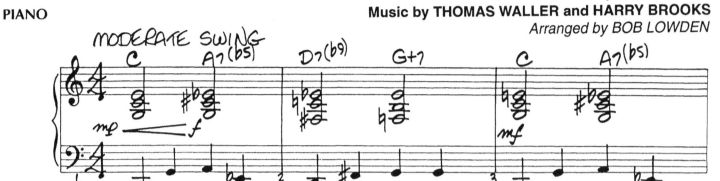

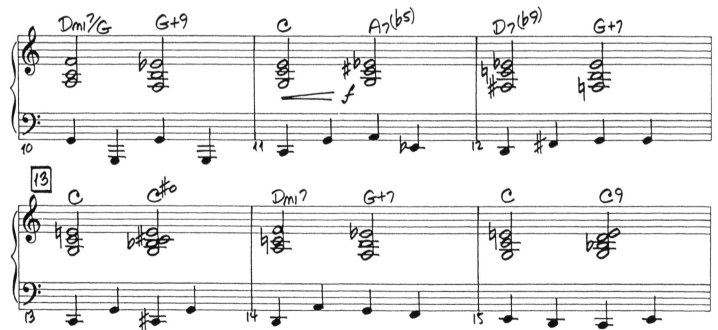

PIANO

ALL THE THINGS YOU ARE
(From VERY WARM FOR MAY)

Lyrics by OSCAR HAMMERSTEIN II
Music by JEROME KERN
Arranged by MICHAEL SWEENEY

PIANO

PIANO

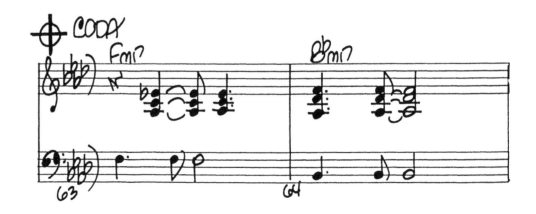

PIANO

BLUE TRAIN
(Blue Trane)

PIANO

By JOHN COLTRANE
Arranged by MICHAEL SWEENEY

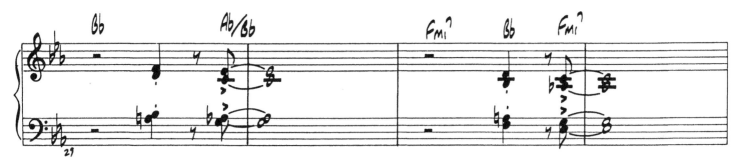

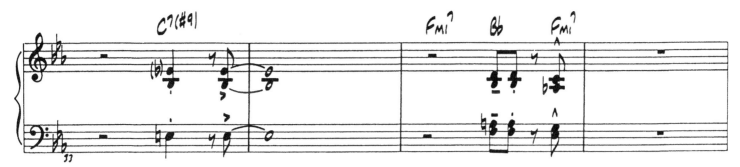

PIANO

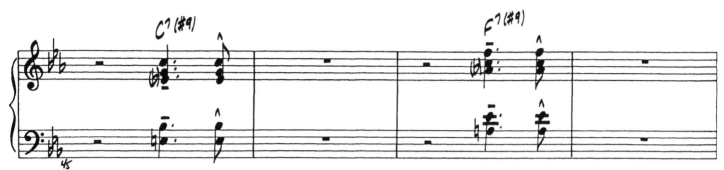

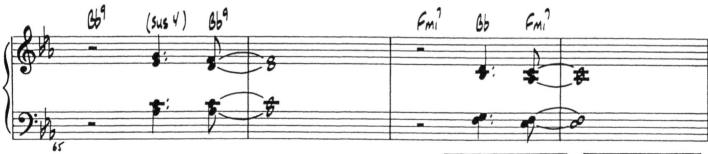

PIANO

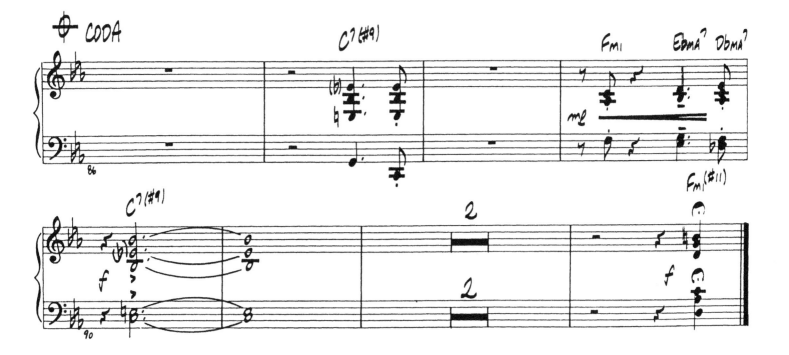

CARAVAN
(From SOPHISTICATED LADIES)

**Words and Music by DUKE ELLINGTON,
IRVING MILLS and JUAN TIZOL**
Arranged by MICHAEL SWEENEY

PIANO

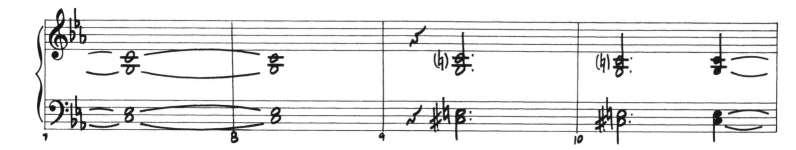

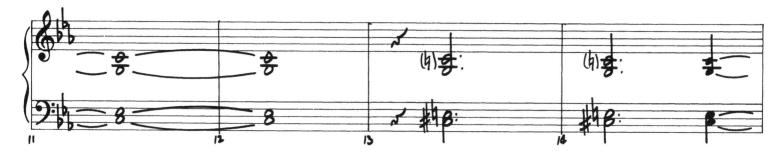

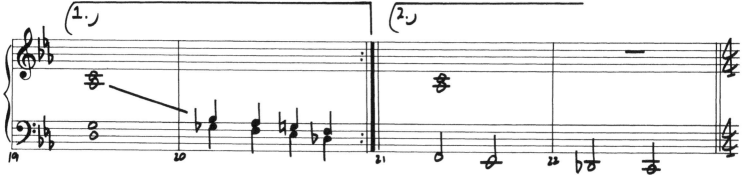

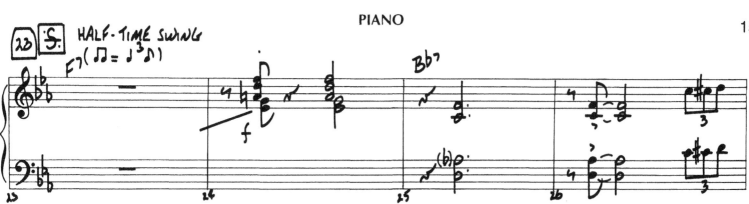

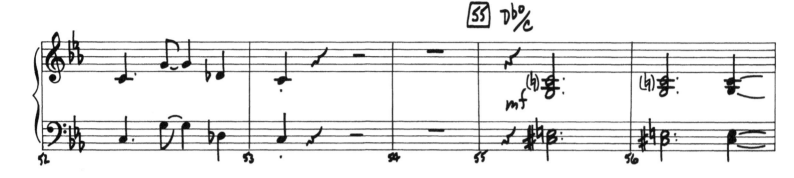

PIANO

CHAMELEON

PIANO

By HERBIE HANCOCK, PAUL JACKSON,
HARVEY MASON and BENNIE MAUPIN
Arranged by MICHAEL SWEENEY

PIANO

PIANO

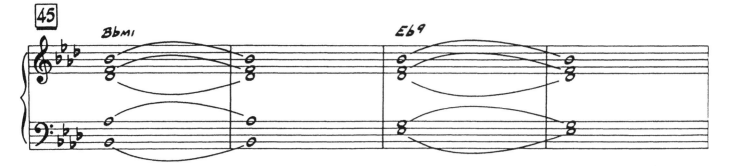

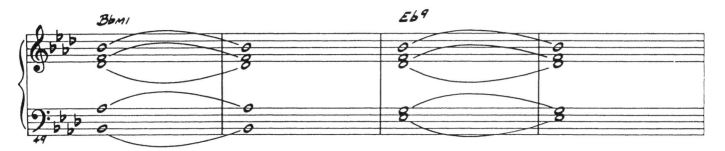

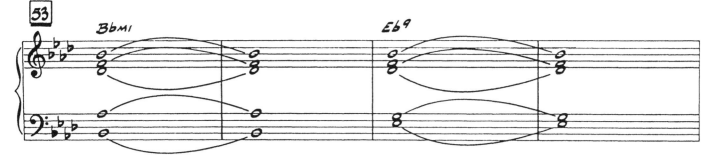

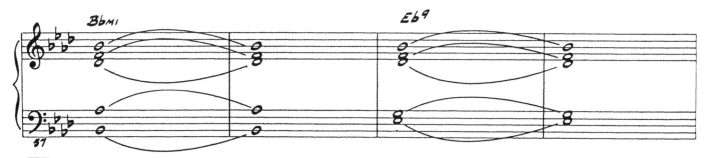

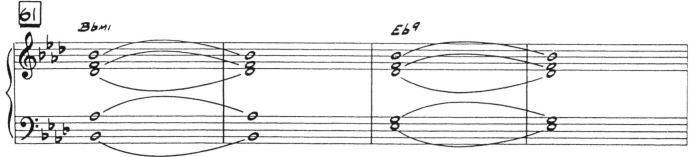

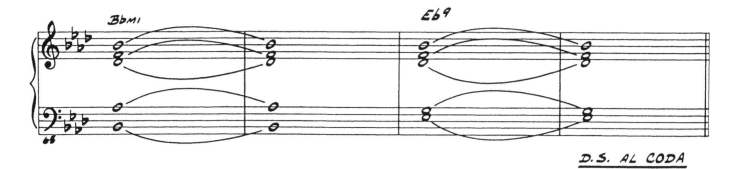

D.S. AL CODA

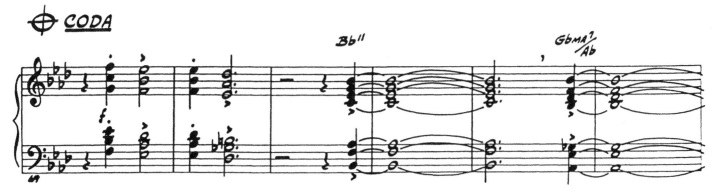

FLY ME TO THE MOON
(In Other Words)

Words and Music by BART HOWARD
Arranged by JERRY NOWAK

PIANO

PIANO

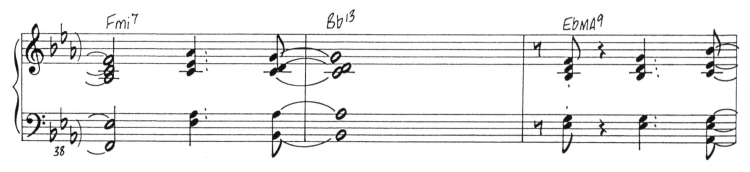

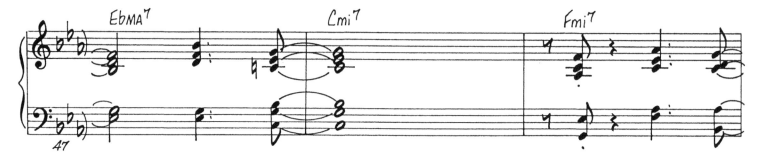

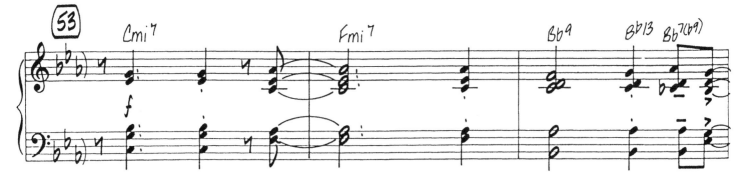

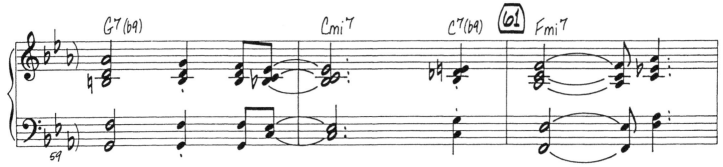

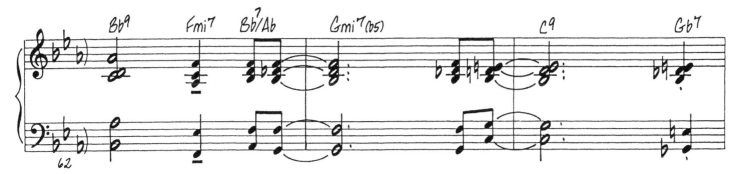

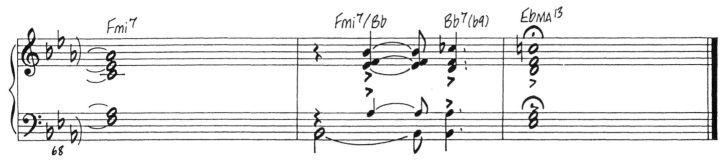

THE GIRL FROM IPANEMA
(Garôta De Ipanema)

PIANO

Original Words by VINICIUS DE MORAES
Music by ANTONIO CARLOS JOBIM
Arranged by JOHN BERRY

PIANO

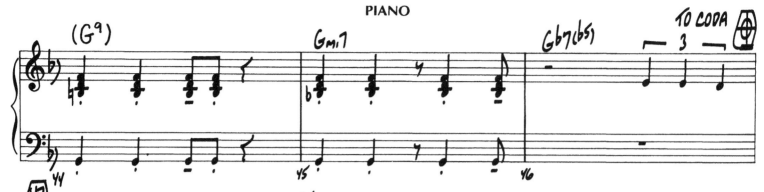

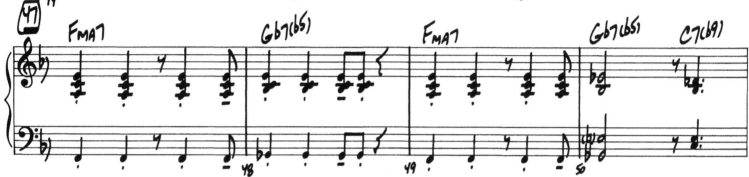

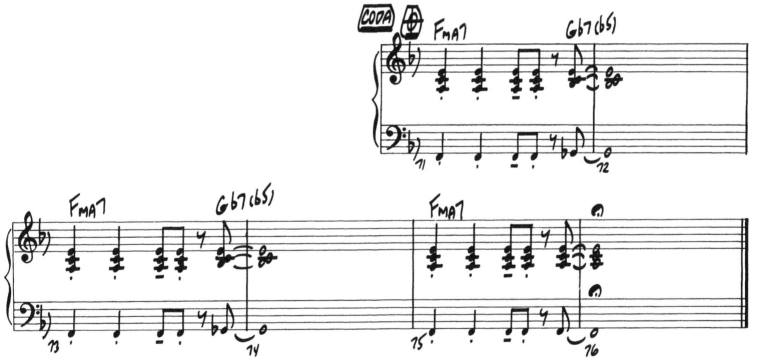

IN THE MOOD

By JOE GARLAND
Arranged by MICHAEL SWEENEY

PIANO

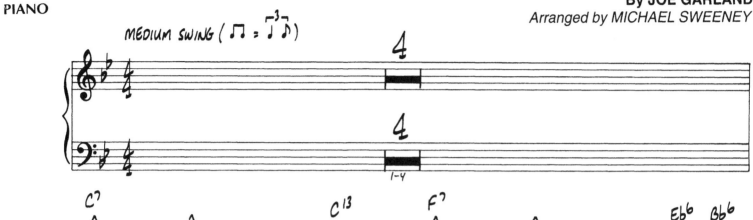

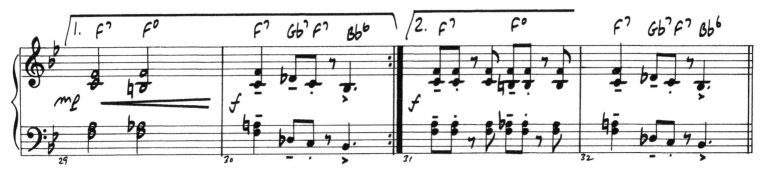

PIANO

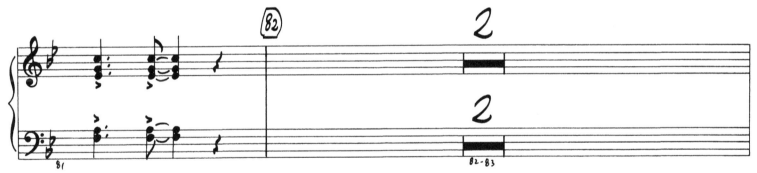

INSIDE OUT

PIANO

By MICHAEL SWEENEY

MILESTONES

By **MILES DAVIS**
Arranged by PETER BLAIR

PIANO

PIANO

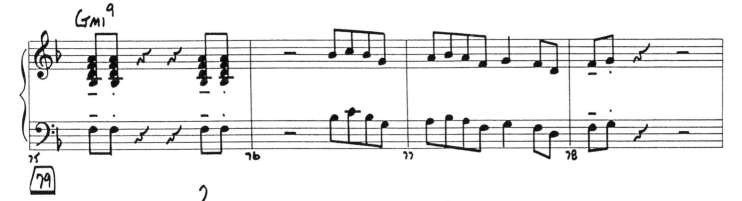

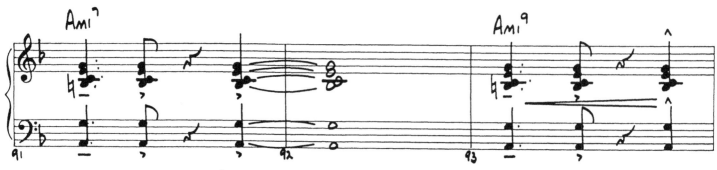

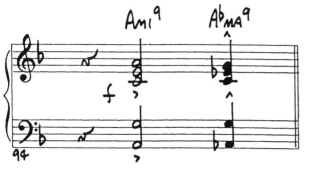

D.S. AL CODA
(W/REPEAT)

A NIGHTINGALE SANG IN BERKELEY SQUARE

Lyric by ERIC MASCHWITZ
Music by MANNING SHERWIN
Arranged by ROGER HOLMES

PIANO

ONE NOTE SAMBA
(Samba De Uma Nota So)

Original Lyrics by NEWTON MENDONCA
English Lyrics by ANTONIO CARLOS JOBIM
Music by ANTONIO CARLOS JOBIM
Arranged by JERRY NOWAK

PIANO

MCA music publishing

PIANO

PIANO

ROUTE 66

PIANO

By BOBBY TROUP
Arranged by MICHAEL SWEENEY

PIANO

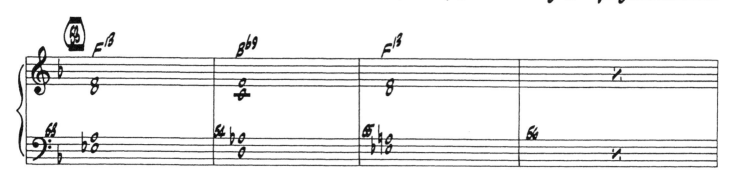

PIANO

ST. LOUIS BLUES

Words and Music by W.C. HANDY
Arranged by MICHAEL SWEENEY

WHEN I FALL IN LOVE

Words by EDWARD HEYMAN
Music by VICTOR YOUNG
Arranged by ROGER HOLMES

PIANO